This book belongs to

Sophia Evenson

THE DOVE AWARD SIGNATURE SERIES

Awesome God

A VERY SPECIAL STORY FOR CHILDREN
BASED ON THE DOVE AWARD™ SONG BY *Rich Mullins*

STORY WRITTEN BY STEPHEN ELKINS · NARRATED BY STEVE GREEN

ILLUSTRATED BY ELLIE COLTON

BROADMAN
&HOLMAN
PUBLISHERS

Nashville, Tennessee

With special thanks to Frank Breeden, Bonnie Pritchard, and the Gospel Music Association.

Song performed by the Wonder Kids Choir:
Emily Elkins, Laurie Evans, Amy Lawrence, Lindsay McAdams,
Amy McPeak, and Olivia Evans
Solo performed by Emily Elkins.

Arranged and produced by Stephen Elkins.
CD recorded in a split-track format.
Recorded at Wonder Workshop, Mt. Juliet, TN

Awesome God, Copyright © 1988 BMG Songs, Inc. (ASCAP),
All rights reserved. Used by permission.

Copyright © 2003 by Stephen Elkins
Published in 2003 by Broadman & Holman Publishers, Nashville, Tennessee

Cover design and layout by Ed Maksimowicz.

Scripture taken from the HOLY BIBLE, NEW INTERNATIONAL VERSION.
Copyright © 1973, 1978, 1984 by International Bible Society.
Used by permission of Zondervan Publishing House. All rights reserved.

A catalog record for this book is available from the Library of Congress.

DEWEY: C781.7
SUBHD: JESUS CHRIST \ POPULAR CHRISTIAN MUSIC--TEXTS

ISBN 0-8054-2664-7

1 2 3 4 5   07 06 05 04 03

How awesome is the Lord
Most High, the great King
over all the earth!
Psalm 47:2

When He rolls up his sleeves, He ain't just puttin' on the ritz. Our God is an awesome God!

"Who can tell me what 'puttin' on the ritz' means?" quizzed Mrs. Barnes. "It means when God decides to do something, it's not just for show," answered Katie. "Very good," said Mrs. Barnes, trying to keep the bus load of anxious kids focused on her and not the terrible storm outside. She and her class were going to Space Central. Just then, a huge thunderclap echoed through the bus, but she continued, "Anyone else know how awesome God is?"

One hand went up in to the air. "OK, Jenny."

There is thunder in His footsteps and lightning in His fists. Our God is an awesome God!

"Thunder in his footsteps?" Jackie blurted out. "Well, He must be running all over heaven right now!" The kids burst into laughter. Boom! Came another clap of thunder, and the laughter stopped.

"Three more miles!" said the bus driver.

"Kids, while you gather up your things, we have time for one more student to tell us how awesome God is," said Mrs. Barnes.

Thinking for a minute Emily said, "First the bad news."

$\mathcal{A}$nd the Lord wasn't jokin' when He kicked 'em out of Eden…

"God created the Garden of Eden as a perfect place for Adam and Eve. It had everything they needed to live. But one day Adam and Eve disobeyed God," Emily explained. "From our study of creation, I remember that their disobedience separated them from God. Because of their sin they had to leave the perfect garden God had created for them. But there's also some good news!"

11

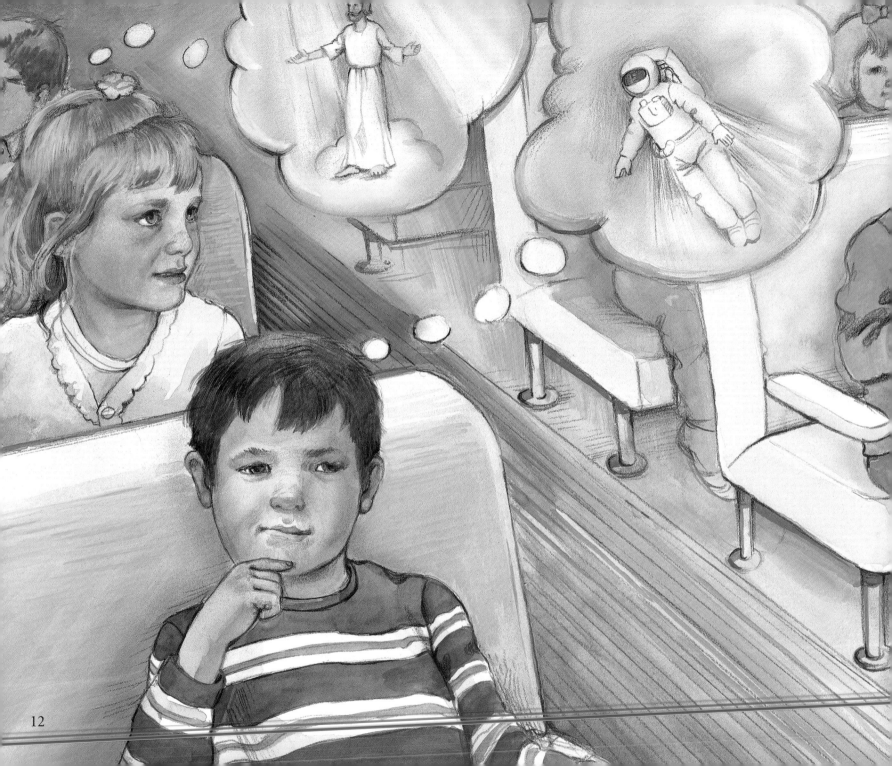

*It wasn't for no
reason that He shed
His blood ...*

AWESOME GOD

"It was part of God's plan to send His only Son, Jesus into this world to save us from sin. Jesus became our bridge back to God.

"That's the good news. " said Emily. "Did Jesus come from outer space?" asked Billy.

"He came from heaven." said Mrs. Barnes. "And when He went back to heaven he rose up into the air."

"In a rocket?" asked Billy. "Not in a rocket," Emily said smiling.

"He went back to heaven without any machines at all, it was a miracle. But that's not all. "

His return is very close and so you'd better be believin' that our God is an awesome God.

"Emily, that was wonderful," encouraged Mrs. Barnes.

Just then Mark shouted, "Look! Rocket ships!" The children, tired from a long drive, burst into chatter, excited to have finally made it to Space Central. It had been a long drive from First Church, but what an exciting way to celebrate spring break!

15

Our God is an awesome God. He reigns from heaven above with wisdom, power, and love. Our God is an awesome God!

"Remember kids, when rockets blast off into outer space, our God is reigning there, too! God is everywhere in this vast universe. So, are we ready to have some fun?" Mrs. Barnes asked her class.

"Yes!" came the shout! The kids cheered as they left the bus. Mrs. Barnes was grateful the storm had passed, "Our first stop is the Planetarium where the stars are projected onto the ceiling," she announced.

*And when the sky
was starless in the void
of the night, our God is
an awesome God.*

AWESOME GOD

Jill, the tour guide, explained, "To reach our second closest star, Alpha Centauri, we would have to travel at the speed of light for over 4 years."

"What's the closest one?" asked Brad.

"Our sun, of course. It's only 93 million miles or eight light minutes from earth. The average star is eight light years from its closest neighbor, and there are billions of stars." Jill continued, "It is hard to imagine how big this universe is!"

Mrs. Barnes whispered, "There was a time when there were no stars in the sky."

He spoke into the darkness and created the light. Our God is an awesome God!

God created each star and placed it in the night sky exactly where He wanted it," Mrs. Barnes continued. Jill pointed out groups of stars called constellations. They had funny names like the Big Dipper, Andromeda, and Orion. Then the group went into the space museum to see photos of the planets.

"The surface of the planet Jupiter is covered with sulfur, which used to be called brimstone." Jill added.

The judgment and wrath He poured out on Sodom.

"That's where I've heard of brimstone," said Sarah.

"According to the Bible the city of Sodom was once covered with brimstone that showered down from the sky. It must have looked a lot like Jupiter, a planet without any life," said Mrs. Barnes.

They all marveled as Jill talked about the many mysteries of the solar system. She said, "Each planet travels around the sun in its own orbit, with the precision of a brand new watch.

The mercy and grace He gave us at the cross,

As the kids finished the tour Mrs. Barnes, said, "Our God, who created a sun that's 15 million degrees centigrade, also created earth and put it just the right distance from the sun so that plant and animal life could exist. God even made an ozone layer to protect us from harmful sun rays.

"Yes," said Emily, "But the most amazing thing He's ever done was to lay down His own life to save you and me?"

25

I hope that we have not too quickly forgotten that our God is an awesome God!

"How could we ever forget that?" exclaimed Brad. "Now, every time we look up into the night sky and see all the constellations, we will be forever amazed at God's awesome power.

"We were just reading in the Psalms where David, the shepherd boy penned these words three thousand years ago, 'The heavens declare the glory of God and the earth, the power of His hands,'" he said.

Our God is an awesome God. He reigns from heaven above with wisdom, power, and love. Our God is an awesome God!

In the exhibition hall, the kids saw moon rocks, meteorites, and working models of the solar system. "How big is the universe?" asked Martha.

"As far as we know it never ends," answered Jill. "And that is one of the greatest mysteries of all."

As they looked at the lunar rovers, space shuttles, and galaxies beyond, they began to see that a universe so complex could only be created by a truly awesome God!

29

Our God is an awesome God! Our God is an awesome God!

AWESOME GOD

"He created a never-ending universe to hold His never-ending love," John proclaimed.

As the tour came to a end, the kids boarded the bus for the journey back home. Mrs. Barnes again asked, "Having learned so much about our solar system today, how awesome is our God?"

Tracy, the youngest, spoke softly, "Our God is so big, He reaches out to the farthest galaxy, yet He's close enough to hear my prayers."

Mrs. Barnes could only add, "Awesome, Tracy, awesome."

Don't miss the other titles in
the Dove Award™ Signature Series for Children

The Great Adventure
Based on the Dove Award™ Song
by Steven Curtis Chapman
0-8054-2399-0

Thank You
Based on the Dove Award™ Song
by Ray Boltz
0-8054-2400-8

God is In Control
Based on the Dove Award™ Song
by Twila Paris
0-8054-2402-4

Testify to Love
Based on the Dove Award™ Song
by Avalon
0-8054-2416-4

I've Just Seen Jesus
Based on the Dove Award™ Song
by Larnelle Harris
0-8054-2665-5

Available at Christian Bookstores everywhere.